Big
Science Ideas

Why do animals become extinct?

Bobbie Kalman

Crabtree Publishing Company

www.crabtreebooks.com

Big

Science Ideas

Created by Bobbie Kalman

for Aidyn Faith Kasper,
a joyful rainbow whose smile brightens the room.
Your light shines through everything you say and do!

**Author and
Editor-in-Chief**
Bobbie Kalman

Editor
Kathy Middleton

Proofreader
Crystal Sikkens

Photo research
Bobbie Kalman

Design
Bobbie Kalman
Katherine Berti
Samantha Crabtree
(logo and front cover)

Print and production coordinator
Katherine Berti

Prepress technician
Katherine Berti

Illustrations
Barbara Bedell: page 13 (top left)
Bonna Rouse: pages 13 (top right), 26, 31

Photographs
BigStockPhoto: page 6 (bottom right)
Wikimedia Commons: U.S. Fish & Wildlife Service:
   page 15 (bottom left); Nicolas Marechal: page
   17 (top right)
All other images by Shutterstock

Library and Archives Canada Cataloguing in Publication

Kalman, Bobbie
   Why do animals become extinct? / Bobbie Kalman.

(Big science ideas)
Includes index.
Issued also in electronic formats.
ISBN 978-0-7787-2774-3 (bound).--ISBN 978-0-7787-2779-8 (pbk.)

   1. Extinct animals--Juvenile literature. 2. Endangered
species--Juvenile literature. 3. Extinction (Biology)--Juvenile
literature. I. Title. II. Series: Kalman, Bobbie. Big science ideas.

QL88.K34 2012   j591.68   C2011-907689-6

Library of Congress Cataloging-in-Publication Data

CIP available at Library of Congress

Crabtree Publishing Company

www.crabtreebooks.com   1-800-387-7650

Printed in Canada/012012/MA20111130

Published in Canada
Crabtree Publishing
616 Welland Ave.
St. Catharines, Ontario
L2M 5V6

Published in the United States
Crabtree Publishing
PMB 59051
350 Fifth Avenue, 59th Floor
New York, New York 10118

Published in the United Kingdom
Crabtree Publishing
Maritime House
Basin Road North, Hove
BN41 1WR

Published in Australia
Crabtree Publishing
3 Charles Street
Coburg North
VIC 3058

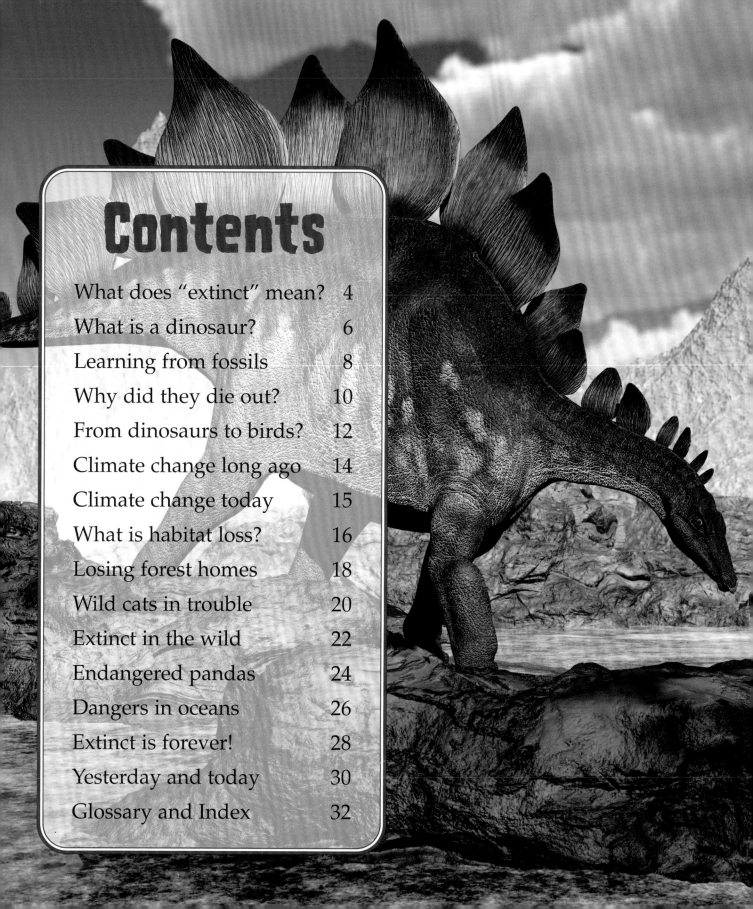

Contents

What does "extinct" mean?

When an animal becomes **extinct**, it has died out or has not been seen in the **wild** for over 50 years. The wild is places that are not controlled by people. Some animals, like dinosaurs, became extinct millions of years ago. Today, thousands of **species**, or types, of animals are in danger of becoming extinct. Many are at risk of dying out in the wild. The chart on the next page explains the words that describe the animals that have become extinct or are in danger of becoming extinct.

This dinosaur was called Triceratops.

Words to know

Scientists use these words to describe animals that are gone or are in danger of disappearing.

extinct (EX) Describes animals that have died out or animals that have not been seen in the wild for at least 50 years

extinct in the wild (EW) Describes animals whose only known living members are in **captivity**, such as at a zoo

critically endangered (CR) Describes animals that are at high risk of dying out in the wild

endangered (EN) Describes animals that are in danger of dying out in the wild

vulnerable (VU) Describes animals that may become endangered because they are facing certain risks

EX

Stegosaurus *dinosaur*

EW

Mexican wolf

CR

baby Sumatran orangutan

EN

Grévy's zebra

VU

polar bear

What is a dinosaur?

Dinosaurs were a group of **reptiles** that lived long ago. Reptiles are animals with **backbones**. Reptiles have **scales**, and they **hatch**, or come out of eggs. There were many kinds of dinosaurs. Some walked on four legs, and others walked on two legs.

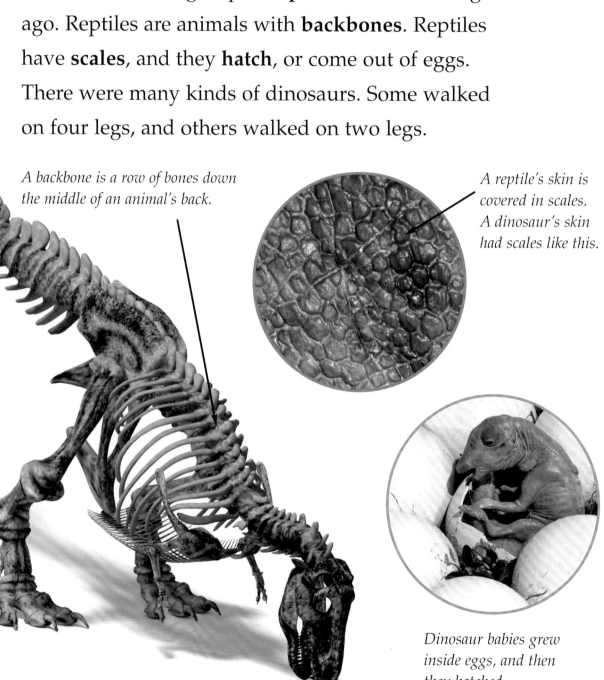

A backbone is a row of bones down the middle of an animal's back.

A reptile's skin is covered in scales. A dinosaur's skin had scales like this.

Dinosaur babies grew inside eggs, and then they hatched.

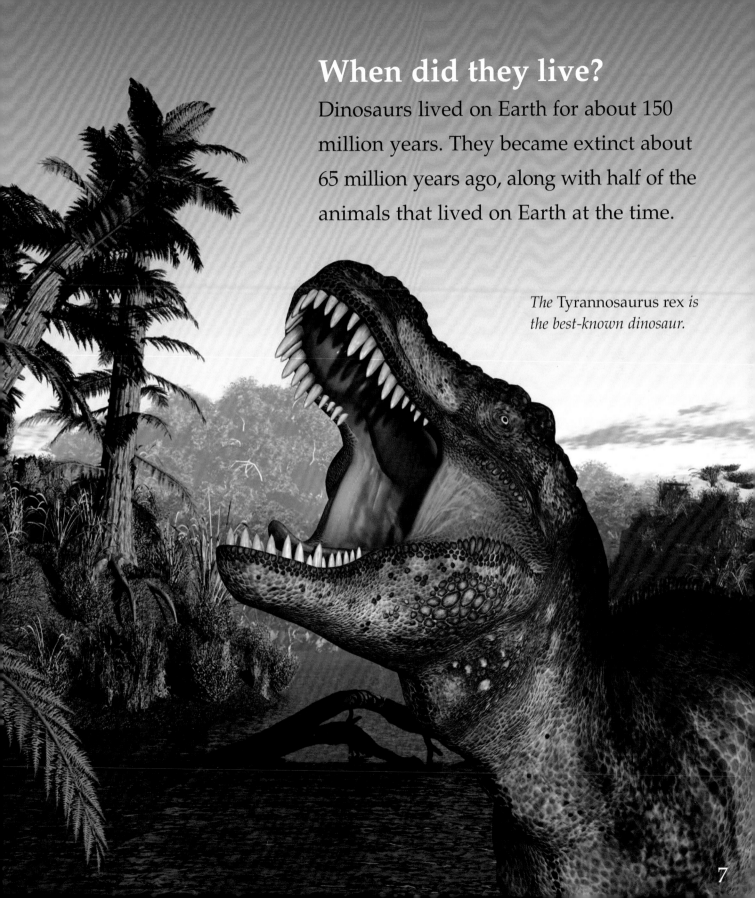

When did they live?

Dinosaurs lived on Earth for about 150 million years. They became extinct about 65 million years ago, along with half of the animals that lived on Earth at the time.

The Tyrannosaurus rex *is the best-known dinosaur.*

Learning from fossils

This body fossil was once part of the head of a Tyrannosaurus rex.

We learn about the lives of extinct animals, such as dinosaurs, from **fossils**. Fossils are traces of plants or animals that lived a long time ago. Some of the dinosaur fossils that have been found are **body fossils**, such as bones, skin, and eggs. **Trace fossils**, such as footprints, show the movements or activities of animals.

This fossil was fixed firmly and totally in rock. It shows all the bones in this animal's body.

Putting it together

Paleontologists are scientists who study animals and plants that lived long ago. Hundreds of different dinosaurs have been identified from fossils. Paleontologists have put together preserved bones to show how dinosaurs may have looked.

This young boy wants to become a paleontologist.

Dinosaur skeletons like these can be seen at museums and science centers.

skeletons

Why did they die out?

No one knows for sure why dinosaurs became extinct, but many scientists believe that one or more **asteroids** were to blame. An asteroid is a big rock that **orbits**, or moves around, the sun. The huge asteroids that hit Earth at that time would have caused wildfires, storms, and volcanic eruptions. A giant dust cloud in the air would have stopped most of the sun's light from reaching Earth.

No food to eat

Plants need sunlight to make food. Without sunlight, plants would have soon died. **Herbivores**, or animals that eat plants, would have starved. **Carnivores**, or animals that eat other animals, would also have died without any herbivores to eat.

asteroid

Ceratosaurus

A big freeze?

Some scientists believe that dinosaurs died out before any asteroids hit. They think that the **climate** all over Earth became much colder, and the dinosaurs could not adjust to the change. Climate is the average weather that an area has had for a long time.

Apatosaurus

From dinosaurs to birds?

Archeopteryx

← *feathers*

Shuvuuia   *tail feathers* →

Many paleontologists believe that not all dinosaurs became extinct. They feel that some dinosaurs changed into birds over time, allowing them to survive after the extinction period. From fossils, scientists discovered a group of small dinosaurs that had hollow bones. The dinosaurs also had legs and feet that looked like those of birds. The scales of these dinosaurs later changed to feathers.

This ostrich, which lives today, looks very much like a Shuvuuia dinosaur. Look at its beak, legs, feet, and tail feathers.

fossil

Archeopteryx

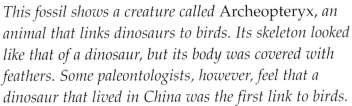

This fossil shows a creature called Archeopteryx, an animal that links dinosaurs to birds. Its skeleton looked like that of a dinosaur, but its body was covered with feathers. Some paleontologists, however, feel that a dinosaur that lived in China was the first link to birds.

Endangered birds today

Some species of **ancient**, or very old, animals may have been able to survive because they changed from reptiles to birds. Many birds today, however, may not be able to survive the changes in the **environment**, or natural world. People cause changes such as pollution and **habitat loss** (see pages 16–17). Whooping cranes, shown on the right, are North American birds that may soon become extinct because they are losing their homes. There are only about 400 of these birds left.

Climate change long ago

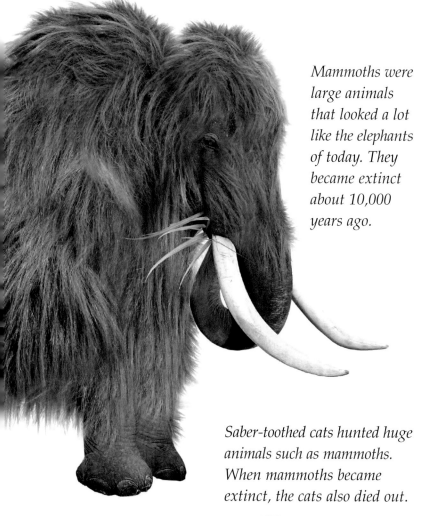

Mammoths were large animals that looked a lot like the elephants of today. They became extinct about 10,000 years ago.

Saber-toothed cats hunted huge animals such as mammoths. When mammoths became extinct, the cats also died out.

Climate includes temperature, wind, and **precipitation**, such as rain or snow. Some scientists feel that as many as 35 types of **prehistoric** animals died out because of **climate change** thousands of years ago. These animals lived millions of years after dinosaurs became extinct. During this time, Earth became warmer, and the foods that were part of the diets of these animals were harder to find. Different kinds of vegetation replaced the foods these giant animals were used to eating. As these herbivores died out, the animals that hunted them also died of starvation.

Climate change today

Scientists believe that a climate change is also happening now, and that Earth is warming up. Even the smallest changes in the temperature on Earth can cause big changes in our environment. Climate change can cause heavier rainstorms and snowstorms, more flooding, and extreme heat. It is hard for plants, animals, and even humans, to **adapt**, or get used to, these changes.

The melting of sea ice is making it difficult for polar bears to hunt seals. Some bears are starving because they cannot find food.

*Warmer temperatures on Earth cause harmful **fungi** to grow on the skin of frogs. Fungi make it difficult for frogs to breathe. The golden toad became extinct in 1989. Many other frogs, such as poison dart frogs, are also critically endangered because of fungi caused by climate change.*

golden toad

poison dart frogs

15

What is habitat loss?

Each year, the number of people on Earth grows, and more food and homes are needed. To grow more food and build more homes, people are taking over the places where wild animals live. Habitat loss is the loss of these natural places. Many animals are becoming endangered because they are losing their homes and their food supply. Animals such as elephants and zebras once lived on large grassy areas called **savannas**. There was plenty of food for them to eat. Today, much of this land is used for farming.

This baby elephant has walked under an electric fence, but its mother would get shocked if she tried to get through. Farmers put up these fences to keep wild animals from eating their crops. Elephants are endangered due to hunting, habitat loss, and lack of food.

Endangered and extinct

Zebras are wild horses that have black and white stripes. There are three kinds of zebras: plains zebras, mountain zebras, and Grévy's zebras. Mountain zebras are vulnerable, and Grévy's zebras are endangered. One kind of zebra, called the quagga, became extinct from being hunted for its meat and hide.

Quaggas were a kind of plains zebra, but they had stripes only on the front of their bodies. Other zebras are striped all over.

Grévy's zebras are the most endangered zebras.

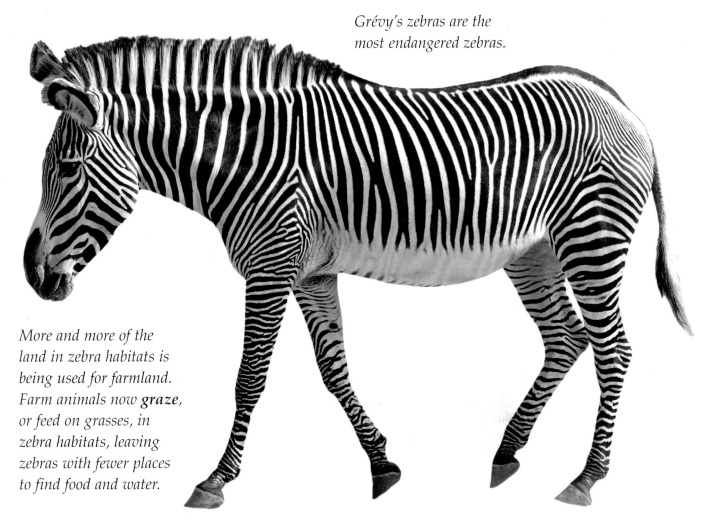

*More and more of the land in zebra habitats is being used for farmland. Farm animals now **graze**, or feed on grasses, in zebra habitats, leaving zebras with fewer places to find food and water.*

17

Losing forest homes

Many forest habitats are cut down each year. The wood is used to build homes, and the land is used for farming. When forests are cut down, animals such as this douc langur monkey lose their homes and food. These monkeys, which live in the rain forests in Asia, are also endangered because of hunting. When people do not have enough food, they hunt and eat wild animals.

Mountain gorillas are apes that live in Africa. They are critically endangered because of habitat loss. They are almost extinct in the wild. They are losing their mountain forest homes and are also being killed for food, just as monkeys are.

Orangutans are orange-colored apes that have lost most of their forest homes. These amazing apes now live only on two islands—Borneo and Sumatra. Both islands are in a country called Indonesia. The Sumatran orangutans are critically endangered. Many Sumatran baby orangutans are being caught and sold as **exotic** pets (see page 29).

Wild cats in trouble

The Javan tiger became extinct in 1980 because of habitat loss and hunting.

Most wild cats are endangered. Some are critically endangered and will become extinct unless people protect them. Wild cats are **predators** that hunt other animals for food. Tigers, leopards, and other wild cats are endangered because of habitat loss. Many are being hunted because they sometimes kill and eat farm animals. People also hunt these cats for their fur and other body parts.

These Sumatran tiger cubs are critically endangered and may soon become extinct in the wild.

Leopards

Leopards are beautiful wild cats with spotted fur. There are eight species of leopards, and all are endangered. Farmers often kill leopards to protect their farm animals from being eaten. Leopards are also hunted for their fur, bones, whiskers, and meat. Many leopards live in **preserves**, or special parks that protect animals.

This Persian leopard cub is endangered.

The Amur leopard is one of the most endangered animals in the world. There are only about 35 of these cats alive in the wild, and they may soon become extinct.

Extinct in the wild

The red wolf is one of two species of wolves in North America. The gray wolf is the other. Red wolves became extinct in the wild in 1980, but a few were raised in captivity, or by people. The wolves that were raised by people were then released into the habitats where they once lived. Now, there are about 300 red wolves, and 120 of them live in the wild.

gray wolf

There are 39 kinds of gray wolves. Some scientists feel the red wolf is really a gray wolf, but others disagree.

The Mexican gray wolf is the smallest type of gray wolf. It is extinct in the wild. It once lived in Mexico, Texas, New Mexico, and Arizona. It was hunted because it ate farm animals.

Red wolves once lived throughout North America in forests and grassy areas called **prairies**. Today, they live only in North Carolina. They are critically endangered and face many challenges.

23

Endangered pandas

bamboo

Giant pandas are supposed to be carnivores, or meat eaters. In fact, they are more like herbivores, or plant eaters. Giant pandas eat almost nothing but a woody plant called bamboo. Many people thought giant pandas were raccoons, but they are part of the bear family. Giant pandas live mainly on mountains in China. They became endangered because bamboo forests are being cut down for farmland and building materials. Most pandas now live on preserves, where they can find food and are protected from hunters.

These pandas are enjoying their bamboo meal at a preserve.

Red pandas

Red pandas belong to their own family of animals, but they are also part of a bigger family that includes skunks, raccoons, and weasels. They are not bears. Red pandas live in the mountains of China, India, and some other countries in Asia. The main threats to red pandas are competition for food with farm animals and habitat loss. Red pandas are also being hunted illegally by **poachers**. They are vulnerable animals.

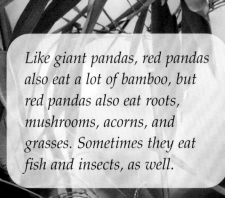

Like giant pandas, red pandas also eat a lot of bamboo, but red pandas also eat roots, mushrooms, acorns, and grasses. Sometimes they eat fish and insects, as well.

Dangers in oceans

The numbers of ocean animals are decreasing, and many are listed as endangered. Whales, dolphins, manatees and dugongs, salmon, sea turtles, and sharks are becoming endangered, some critically endangered. Many of these animals are hit by boats or caught in fishing nets. Ocean creatures are even more vulnerable to problems such as habitat destruction and hunting or fishing. Oil spills and other kinds of pollution are also huge dangers.

*leatherback
sea turtle*

*hawksbill
sea turtle*

*Kemp's ridley
sea turtle*

All sea turtles are endangered, but the hawksbill, Kemp's ridley, and leatherback sea turtles are critically endangered. Today, major threats to sea turtles include loss of nesting areas, pollution, and getting tangled in fishing nets.

All manatees are endangered. Many get caught in fishing nets. Others are killed by boats or die from pollution. These manatees live in the waters around Florida. They are West Indian manatees.

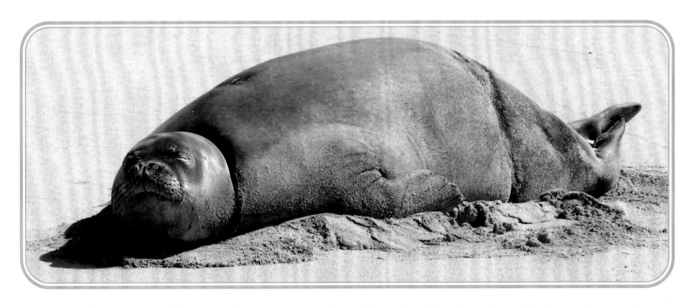

The Hawaiian monk seal lives in the ocean around the Hawaiian Islands. It is critically endangered. These monk seals are often killed by sharks. Many others are dying from diseases. To protect these seals, people are not allowed to go near them while they are resting on the beaches.

Extinct is forever!

When animals become extinct, they are gone forever from Earth. We cannot do anything to save the animals that went extinct long ago, but we can help stop the animals of today from becoming extinct. If everyone made just one change in his or her life, the result could be huge! Telling people about why animals become endangered and extinct is a great place to start. Here are some other simple things we can do.

Do not buy bottled water. Drink filtered tap water from a glass or a reusable drink container. Water bottles end up in lakes and oceans and have been found in the stomachs of many dead animals, including dolphins, sea turtles, and seabirds. Plastic does not break down!

Some parrot species are critically endangered because people trap the parrots to be sold as pets. Many of the birds die on the way to their new homes. In other cases, when pet birds are set free, they have babies in the wild and take over the food supply of the **native species** that live in the area. They also eat the crops that people grow. The monk parakeet from South America, for example, became a popular pet in several U.S. states and some European countries, but some now consider them pests. You and your classmates can help educate people about not buying or releasing exotic pets such as birds, snakes, monkeys, or apes.

Cars use gasoline, which causes pollution, which causes climate change. Use a bike or scooter to go places, instead of asking your parents to drive you. To help clean the air even more, plant some trees in your community.

Yesterday and today

Some extinct animals look very much like animals that are alive today. Match the animals that look alike to you. The extinct animals are on this page, and the animals that are alive today are on the opposite page. Give reasons for your choices.

saber-toothed cat

Zuniceratops

Shuvuuia

Macrauchenia

mammoth

How are the animals on this page similar to the animals on the opposite page? How are they different?

white rhinoceros

cougar

giant anteater

ostrich

Asian elephant

Glossary

Note: Some boldfaced words are defined where they appear in the book.

adapt To become different to suit a new habitat

captivity A state of living in an enclosed area, such as a zoo, and being raised by people

carnivore An animal that eats other animals

climate change A change in the long-term weather conditions in an area

crops Plants that are grown by people to be eaten as food

exotic Something that is not naturally found in an area

fossil A living thing, or mark made by a living thing, that has hardened into rock over time

fungi Single-celled organisms that feed on other living things, causing illness and sometimes death

habitat loss When the natural place where an animal lives is destroyed

herbivore An animal that eats mainly plants

native species An animal or plant that is naturally found in a particular place or area

poacher A hunter who hunts and kills animals that are against the law to hunt

precipitation Any form of water, such as rain or snow, that falls to the Earth's surface

prehistoric Describing animals that existed before the beginning of recorded history

preserve A natural area set aside by a country's government to protect the plants and animals living in that area

scale A small, flat, tough structure on the skin of some animals, such as fish and reptiles

wild The natural places where animals live

Index